Philosophy for children

From child to children

Once upon a time!

Daddy from heaven sent it!

Coloring story!

By: Bernardo Octaviano Pereira

This book belongs to:

____

I dedicate this work, firstly, to my parents who I love so much, to my teachers, to my dear aunts and to all my friends, may God bless you all infinitely!

Bernardo Octaviano Pereira

06/04/2024

Once upon a time, in a small village surrounded by lush green mountains, there lived a woman who cared for her family with love and affection, but faced difficult times.

The pickings had been slim and the shelves of his modest pantry were bare. She looked at her children with sadness, as she had no food to put on their tables.

One day, the woman looked up at the sky and, with a mournful sigh, whispered a silent prayer to the "daddy in heaven",

ordering a food basket for your family. With hope in her heart, she continued her daily tasks, trusting that her words would be heard.

To his
surprise and
relief, not long
passed before
a kind
messenger
knocked on
his door.

The messenger held a large basket filled with fresh fruits, vegetables and bread. The woman's eyes filled with tears of gratitude as she accepted the generous offer.

"Thank you, Father in heaven, for listening to my prayers," murmured the woman, her lips trembling with emotion. However, before the man left, he hesitated for a moment and revealed the truth behind delivering the basket.

"Ma'am," he said in a soft voice, "it wasn't daddy from heaven who sent me these foods. It was the bad bug."

A chill ran down the woman's spine upon hearing those words, but she refused to let fear consume her. With a firm determination, she looked into the man's eyes and said:

"It doesn't matter where this help came from. When Daddy from heaven commands, even the bad animal is obliged to obey." The man was impressed by the woman's wisdom and courage. He left, leaving the woman with her basket of food,

In the days that followed, the story of the woman's generosity and unwavering faith spread throughout the village. The villagers, touched by the woman's courage and inspired by her kindness,

came together to help. They planted new seeds in the fields, shared their own harvests, and ensured that no family went hungry.

And so, even in the face of the most challenging circumstances, kindness and generosity prevailed in that small village. The woman, with a smile on her face and gratitude in her heart, knew that as long as there was love and solidarity between people, they would always find a way to overcome any adversity.

The end!